FINDING GOD'S WILL FOR YOU

Leading a Guided Life

Ray W. Lincoln

Copyright 2006, printed in Blenheim, New Zealand
Copyright 2008, printed in the United States of America
Copyright 2020, printed in the United States of America

ISBN: 978-0-9996349-6-7

Apex Publications
Ingram, TX

Dedicated to the memory of my mother whose concern that I find God's will for my life and whose teachings that formed my early mind are among my most treasured gifts.

"He will guide you with His eye," Psalm 32:8

ACKNOWLEDGMENTS

Thanks to my wife, Mary Jo, who has labored without complaint in typing and proofing, but with the occasional "You won't say that, will you?" guidance. I can't do without her wisdom.

I am also grateful to two people, Alister and Joanne Bell, who first heard about my venturing again (this time in my "retirement") into the world of writing, and who provided the backing for the original production of this booklet. Their recognition of a possible ministry that might help people in their stress has endeared them to my heart.

Finally, I wish to thank Vicar Richard Elena who provided encouragement and actively worked to remove obstacles that could have prevented the production of this booklet.

Ray W. Lincoln

Contents

Introduction

Since I'm not the expert on finding God's will, let me introduce you to the expert who knows all you need to know. His wisdom is beyond repute and you will not be led astray.

God is his name.

In the two "books" he has given us is all the guidance we need for finding that life of unsurpassed happiness, the life designed for us and implanted in our makeup when we were created. In addition, he has provided the personal direction via his built-in spirit-internet that saves us and guides our decisions on a daily basis.

With this kind of radar, we can find our way in the darkest of times.

Oh, the two books? You will have to read on to find the answer if you haven't guessed them already. You won't be kept in suspense for long!

FINDING GOD'S WILL FOR YOU — GUIDED LIVES AND THE ROLE OF FAITH

(A Reasoned Approach to the Practice of Our Faith)

Have you ever wanted God to appear in front of you and write his will clearly on paper — in English? Yes, and sign it too? Oh, and give you a notarized copy?

Particularly when stress and worry drain all the joy out of our lives and we are reduced to a fearful, crippled crawl, most of us find it a somewhat pressing urge to know God's will. If only we could know for sure, on demand, that an all-powerful God had given his blessing to our decisions, life would be a lot less unnerving. I think we can.

It's not "cool" to talk about needing God these days. But a recent survey in the United States highlighted the fact that the majority of people still pray when they are in serious trouble. So we have plenty of company. Of course, in admitting our need of reassurance, we are also confessing our dependence on God — a God who is, fortunately, gracious and (surprise!) already helping us before we even ask.

Guidance Is on God's Terms

First We Must Learn: We can't dictate how God will speak to us.

When you ask for God's guidance, don't expect to dictate to God how he should reply as Gideon did. Gideon asked God to make the fleece Gideon put outside wet and the ground around it dry the first morning. Then he asked God, on the next morning, to make the ground wet and the fleece dry, — just to be sure he was hearing God's message correctly. (You can read the exciting story in Judges 6:36ff.) God's kindness in reassuring Gideon's weak faith on Gideon's terms was an exception to the norm.

This booklet is designed to help you use God's normal terms for finding His will.

Next Learn: There will always be something mysterious

God Himself is a mystery. And the final word on everything mysterious will not be written until we meet God one day and understand all about his ways — ways that are unexplainable to us now in the language and experience of this earthly life.

For humans to understand God would be like asking an ant to understand a human. Our minds are far too small to grasp everything there is to know about his ways. We'll try to demystify some things; but we'll have to wait for a full understanding.

The Relationship Between Mystery and Faith

Mystery is an important element in our lives. Being limited beings, we look mystery in the face every day. But there is another reason for the mysterious. God means for his methods of communication to be, in part, a mystery. Does that surprise you?

It's not that he wants to keep us in the dark and maintain dominance over comparatively ignorant creatures. He wants us to learn all we can. The reason for his not disclosing his methods to us is in one word: faith. Faith and mystery (what we just can't understand) are closely related in our relationships with God – partners, you could say, that are always holding hands, inseparable. Faith is the only path to God. And that path enters the mysterious realm of the spirit — both God's Spirit and our spirit. Faith is the key that enables us to experience the mystery of God — his love, grace, and power.

Here's the close tie between these inseparable twins: when there is no mystery, there is no need for faith. No faith, and the door to spiritual reality remains closed. One depends on the other.

By their nature, spiritual things cannot be examined by science. How can science put, let's say, God's thoughts into a test tube as though they were some kind of "matter" and examine them? How can science know what the thoughts of a spiritual being are in the first place? You can't examine what you don't know. So when entering the spiritual world we need faith, not science.

Except when God wants to dramatically get our attention, a relationship with him is always a matter of our believing in him in order that the reality of his care and presence can be felt. You will read a lot about faith in the following pages because we "live by faith". "Without faith, it is impossible to please God, for he who comes to God must believe that he exists...," Hebrews 11:6. Faith, then, will play a large part in our finding the will of God for our lives.

Next Learn: Our lives are guided without our asking

We lead guided lives. So there is a sense in which God takes care of this matter of directing us without our conscious concern.

If God is interested in our welfare, he has to be involved somehow — watching what is happening to us and making decisions about what he will allow and what he won't.

The ancient phrase, "He will guide you with his eye," (Psalm 32: 8) is a poetic way of saying God will direct you with his complete knowledge (omniscience). We can't see God's eye to see which way he is looking, or see through his eye to know what he is seeing. God will do the seeing for us without our knowing that he is doing it. And since he sees everything that is happening and knows everything that is about to happen, we can feel secure when surrendered to his leadership. Jesus made this point by pointing out that the lilies and birds don't worry; they just live. Do the same as the birds. Trust in his constant guidance all the time under all circumstances. This is the first lesson to learn if you want to find his will for you.

The maze of this life is full of uncertainties. Life is one big risk. You have a choice of guides — God, friends, human gurus or yourself. Choose your guide and trust him. My choice is the same as the Psalmist's, "Guide me with your eye, Lord." I'd rather trust God than any lesser authority.

In taking this attitude, we take the stress out of our lives and reap the benefits of trusting God. The alternative is worry — lots of it at times! Break the addiction to worry and become addicted to faith. They are opposite ways of living. It is impossible to live both ways at the same time. Oh, and when we do, we'll have a lot less questions to ask.

Do We Believe God Is In All That Happens to Us?
It is our lack of confidence in trusting his promised leading that makes us ask for him to speak to us and reassure us at times. Since he has promised to lead us, why should we be afraid, or confused, or desire more assurance? Answer: because we are human (limited beings who can't know everything). This cry for confirmation is normal for a faith in its journey of development. It's also because we have doubts that weaken our faith and make us long for the certainty that

wobbly faith can't give us. "All we, like sheep, have gone astray" and must find our way back to the path. So what do we want more than to hear his voice again saying, "This is the way; walk in it?"

Does this question come to mind? "Why don't we forget asking for his will since he is looking after us anyway?" Because he has given us something called free will and has also given us a challenge, as creatures made in his image, to be responsible with our choices. Since we have to make most of our decisions, we need to know if our decisions are right and where he wants us to go.

Still, it's such a pity that we don't believe more strongly that our faith in God is our greatest reassurance. And we fail to continue to believe whenever the pressures are on, don't we?

If you have a passion for doing God's will and you admit your humanness and your weak faith, this booklet is for you. God has graciously granted us some walking sticks to lean on.

God Will Speak to Us?

Next, We Must Ask: Can I expect God to speak to me?

As far as Adam, Eve, Abraham, Moses (and the list is very long) are concerned, God spoke to them. So we are going to ask, "Could I expect him to speak to me either audibly or in a voice that only I can hear?" Consider the evidence...

A Very Talkative God
He seems bent on talking to us. And talking, for him, can mean he talks through the words of the Bible, his acts of creation (how gloriously he talks through a flower!), his chosen prophets, dreams, his preachers, his still small voice in our minds, his audible instructions. And let's not forget, he talks through circumstances if we believe that everything that happens to us is either allowed to happen or willed to happen by God. Some of his communications we welcome more than others. We don't particularly rave over a "No" or a "You'll just have to wait." By the way, he never answers, "I'm not listening."

Conclusion? A very talkative God, indeed! Why is it that people keep saying, "If only God would say something and make his presence felt?" He's making his presence felt everyday, all day. It's just when we fail to remember or believe he is talking to us that we fail to hear his voice in all that is happening to us and around us. When a bird sings, do we hear a pretty song or an uplifting melody of praise? Do we hear a song at all?

For me, with a philosophical background, it is arresting to hear Jesus called "The Word," John 1:1. This was a philosophical designation used by the Greeks, meaning the very expression or voice of God. Jesus is the very expression and voice of God to us in all he does and says. Now can you see how important it is for us to have a working knowledge of the life and teachings of Jesus? Everything Jesus did and said is the voice of God in understandable human terms being heard here in our world. God is talking again — this time in Jesus!

Don't forget, he can talk through you, too. Be God's voice to others.

Now Learn: God wants to participate with us in a two-way conversation.

We are urged by Jesus to talk to God in prayer and God will answer us. "Everyone who asks, receives," Matt 7: 8. Which means, at the very least, God is bound by the integrity of that promise to reply when we pray. He has to reply or destroy his claim to honesty and reliability.

Do we understand that God is conditioned by his own moral being? Simply put: who he is binds him to be what he is. So, if God is absolutely trustworthy, trusting him to keep his promise is the safest thing we humans can do. This is the only real certainty in a very uncertain world.

Because of this constant encounter with uncertainty in our lives, our minds have become skeptical of everything — even the promises of God. We come to believe that to live by faith in God's promises is a shaky, risky way of living. Nothing could be further from reality.

Recently, a man and his wife were put on trial for apparently neglecting medical help and, instead, trusting God to cure their sick baby. Now I believe that if they were aware of their baby's need of help, they were bound to use all of the medical help available to them as well as to pray and trust God for their child's healing. But the thing that stood out to me was the attitude of the reporter who, reflecting the spirit of our age, cast doubt on the sanity of people who would have such a reliance on prayer. "Who would want to pray when you can go to the doctor," was the misinformed attitude. Rather, who in their right mind would forget to pray on the way to the doctor when God, not the doctor, is the ultimate healer?

God can be trusted! Yes, but it seems trusting God is the most difficult lesson we have to learn.

This commitment by God to answer all our prayers leads to the most exciting aspect of prayer, don't you think? Checking the mailbox, I mean. Do you? (See under the section below, "Ask — and Receive a Reply," for instructions on checking the mailbox.)

So should I expect him to talk to me? Yes! In fact I would go so far as to say that if you don't hear him talk to you, you are missing out on one of life's great daily events.

The saddest day in a human's existence is the day that human doesn't, in one way or another, hear God speak to them. The second saddest day could be the day they forget to talk to God. God wants us to talk to him and he wants us to listen for his voice.

Is Every Claim to Have Heard God's Voice Valid?
We often hear people say, "God spoke to me and said…" Did he really, or were they just imagining he did? Sometimes we wonder. Perhaps they heard their own wishes ringing in their heads and, only too willingly, came to the happy conclusion that it was God speaking to them.

Every time we hear someone claim to have heard God's voice, should we believe them? Is it possible to be self-deceived? Well, reason it this way: Every shaft of light has its shadow; every good thing is highlighted by the bad things, and in this unlikely way, even the devil and all evil is forced to serve the purpose of God by highlighting his truthfulness. Evil can't exist without making us aware of how good God is. It was good, not evil, that was the image in which we were originally created; and to "good's" powerful existence evil (the shadow) points an unwilling finger.

So, should we expect to find misunderstandings and misidentifications of God's voice? Sure. Confusion is common.

But the fact that God is talking to us is more common because he talks in so many ways, as we have already discovered.

Fortunately though, we are not required to judge people and their experiences. I would hate to have that task, knowing that since I am a limited space-time creature I simply don't have access to all the facts, and my judgments would be sure to be in error much of the time. Leave the task of judgment to God and enjoy the real experience of God's voice yourself. Again, observe the fake experiences of life, but don't let yourself be compulsively focused on the negatives in others if you want spiritual health.

Does God Speak Audibly to Us All the Time?
No. On rare occasions in the Bible, God's voice is said to be an audible voice. More often, he has been observed to speak to someone while those standing nearby heard nothing. In other words, he spoke inside their minds. On other occasions, we read words like, "God spoke to Abraham and said…" It doesn't say he spoke audibly or in a manner heard only by Abraham. It doesn't tell us how God spoke to Abraham. It just says he spoke to Abraham, with no indication of method. Therefore, it is wise not to claim that God spoke audibly to Abraham on this occasion when the Bible doesn't say he did. It is a basic rule of interpretation, applicable to any piece of literature, that you do not add details to what is said. We know God spoke; but how he spoke is not told to us.

How Does God Talk to Us? We will find several answers — each important. We have already learned God speaks through our circumstances, but there is so much more.

He Speaks In the Details of Our Personal Makeup
Every snowflake, every fingerprint, every voice pattern is unique in its design. Marvelous isn't it. To think that the creator has put so much detail into his creation staggers thought.

We are carefully crafted from the day of our conception and fitted out in every detail, spiritually and physically, for the very life God intended us to live. We have the best genes God could give us to become the greatest he plans for us to be. (Genes are overrated these days because in the infancy of our discoveries about the part they play in forming our uniqueness, we have not paused to consider the mountain of undiscovered evidence that the interaction of spirit and belief, to name only two areas, may have upon their impact on our lives.) Not only genes, also personality and spirit (we're not likely to find a gene for our spirit) — literally everything about us prepares us for what he has in store for us.

Of course, it follows that everything we can learn about ourselves is helpful in our discovery of his plans for us. Learn everything you can about yourself!

Now if you don't know the unique you, you may make the mistake of trying to live for goals that don't fit your makeup or plans that could frustrate and even destroy your potential.

God speaks with deliberation in each unique creation's makeup.

The reading of who we are is sometimes a little confusing. For example, we may lack the physical ability to do something and conclude that God does not intend for us to do it. But he may intend for us to rise above our physical handicap if he plants in us the strong passion to do so. So the reading of God's plan in our makeup must be done with care. As always, it is only part of the puzzle, not the whole.

He Speaks Over an Intangible Internet, Unique to God's Spirit

We know he created us with bodily sense gates — sight, hearing, taste, touch, smell — to soak up the messages from the world around us. But not having a body himself, he also created us with ways for his spirit (which he is) to be able to communicate with our spirit. It is a spiritual way of communicating that does not rely on hearing or seeing or touching, etc.

He has programmed us to receive direct messages from himself — a sort of "spirit e-mail" between spirits. As I read recently in a secular magazine (where the author was summarizing our knowledge of our spiritual makeup), "We are discovering that we are hard-wired for God," he said. He was meaning we have a direct, permanent connection with God (to who this God was he would not commit). Well, let's not say "hard-wired." Let's say whatever you call "a direct link between spirits." An "intangible internet" will do.

And this is the usual way he talks to us: by spirit e-mail. So, without speaking audibly or appearing visibly, he can still very effectively post his message directly onto the screens of our minds and plant feelings in our emotional systems. As a result, he can make us feel things and think things and leave the choice of what we are going to do up to us... if we are reading our e-mails, of course.

Add to this the fact that he alone knows what we are thinking or feeling even before we think or feel it, and you have a God who can help at any moment and prepare us prior to our emergencies. This is only real if we are willing to believe in such a God and his in-built communication system — and use it. We will simply call this method an inner voice.

"Ah," you say, "inner voice." Sounds to me like intuition. It also sounds like that phrase that is so misapplied today: "follow your heart." Beware! You could be thinking dangerously. Both phrases are good in themselves but are subject to easy misinterpretation.

Don't follow your heart as though your heart is the source of your guidance, nor follow your intuitive feelings because you think they are your ultimate source of truth. Follow God's heart beating in your heart. There's a crucial difference. Follow someone more knowledgeable and wiser than yourself. Therefore, don't look inside for your feelings to guide you unless you can identify those feelings as coming from God.

When you have an intuitive feeling, ask if it is the kind of intuition that God could be sending via his intangible internet. If so, follow it.

This inner voice is not the same as conscience, either. Conscience is the sum of the values we have loaded into our memory banks, plus the innate urges that God has preloaded into the mind and heart of every human. It's a real mixture. We are not talking about programmed, software-like conscience when we refer to God's voice. Rather, we are talking about the un-programmed message that he can mysteriously flash onto our mental screens. He's the good and perfect hacker who breaks into our mental computer to give us important messages. He doesn't use a virus to do so, but rather his own program, which he slipped into our software at our creation.

The Mystery He built Into Our Human System

His secret way into our minds is more mysterious than our imagination — as mysterious as that is! Exactly how he does it is the part that is completely unknown. It is the interaction of spirit (God's Spirit) with the physical world of body (our body) via our human spirit.

We are a marvel of physical engineering (body) and spiritual power (spirit) blended together in a baffling and unimaginable way. He alone holds the blueprints and knows the secret entrances. So, if we are designed for God to be able to speak directly to our inner selves, it's now time to find out our part in this adventure for which we have been made.

OUR PART IN DISCOVERING GOD'S LEADING IN OUR LIVES

Having learned how he speaks to us, we need to ask, "What is my part in hearing God's voice?" Let me suggest four steps.

Step One: What has God already said to me?

The first step is to recognize and accept that God may have already spoken to me about whatever it is that is now a concern to me.

God is way ahead of us in his active guiding of our lives, ahead of our prayers — even ahead of our conscious need of direction. Remember, he has already laid a plan for our lives in the gifts and talents, the personality and passions with which we were created. So, our part in his guidance for our lives often starts with a rediscovery of who we are — who we were created to be. Every believer in God should have a consuming interest in who they are and how God has created and equipped them. This means an interest in all gifts, both spiritual and natural, that God has given them.

So always ask first: "What has he equipped me to be and do?" It may be that I need only to ask this question.

I also find most people are confused about what God wants them to do largely because they have no belief in the concept (as we discussed earlier) that we lead guided lives.

Nothing happens to us without God allowing it to happen. That's a rule of faith. Sometimes he must allow the foolish decisions of our free will simply because he has granted us free will. But even then, he will guide us out of our foolish choices — if we let him — while, at the same time, we take responsibility for our actions or lack of action.

Freedom can be good and bad for us: good, when we explore the riches of responsibility and creativeness God has given us; and bad, when we use our freedom to go our way and reject God's wisdom, thus ending up in a quagmire of trouble.

Either way, he is at work in everything for our potential good, even in the bad things that happen to us. Therefore, every circumstance, in that sense, is "in his will" and becomes part of his plan to bring us to our best. He is using even our mistakes to make us better. We must focus first on this truth — that we lead guided lives — and truly accept that belief.

This accepting of our circumstances (Paul's contentment, Philippians 4: 11) and believing that God is at work in everything for our good frees us to live happily and productively.

Step Two: Use your head — It's a gift from God.

The second step is simply a conclusion drawn from the first step. It is not difficult to believe that one of the things God has given us is a brain — maybe hard to find and sometimes on vacation, but nonetheless an integral part of us.

So use your head! Think! It appears that Paul relied heavily on this step in his discovery of God's will for his life. How did he know where to go on his missionary journeys? On occasions, he seems to have felt the Holy Spirit's promptings. On others, it appears that he goes to the next most likely town based on human reasoning. He trusted in the "guided life principle" and the use of the gift God had given him: his brain. There is nothing unspiritual about using your head

The dramatic story of his being redirected to Macedonia is very instructive. He was on his way to the northern inhabitants of Asia Minor (modern Turkey) — since it was a logical next step to complete his penetration into this country — when we are told God threw a "stumbling block" in his way (a very good enigmatic translation of the Greek phrase used in Acts 16:7). What the stumbling block was, we are not told — nor do we need to know. But it caused him to stop and retreat. That night God gave him a special redirection by appearing to him in a dream and calling him to Macedonia.

It is as though God said, "Paul your thinking was good; but there's something your thinking could not have told you, and that is that I need you to forsake your coverage of Asia Minor and go to Macedonia."

Whenever our honest thinking misleads us, God is bound to speak to us and reveal what our thinking could not tell us. He did this on this occasion and he will do this on every necessary occasion. It may be by a dream, but more commonly it will be by an inner conviction that simply has no other explanation to us than a voice from God.

The idea that all of our thinking is tainted by our sinfulness, and, therefore, suspect, is not biblical. When I think, "I must trust God," that thought is hardly sinful. Jesus teaches us to think that way. Again I must emphasize, using your brain is not sub-spiritual. Our thinking mechanisms are, therefore, a real God-given tool for the discovery of God's will.

I like to say, "Do your homework first. Weigh the facts, probabilities and opportunities; and come to the best conclusion. Then, listen in prayer to hear if God is trying to say something else to you. If you are open to God speaking to you, you will not miss his direction."

One more thing that pertains to Step Two: you can only steer a moving vehicle. You are the vehicle; and if you are parked, waiting to be turned in the right direction, you will simply remain undirected and in the location where you currently are. Get moving. Start doing all that you need to do to come to a decision. In the process, God will guide you. Start your engine, put your life in gear, and move. Even God can't turn us in the right direction when we are parked with the engine off!

The disciples had to wait and remain parked where they were for the coming of the Holy Spirit at Pentecost. But after he came, there was no waiting (parking) required. Waiting for God's will to be revealed (which seems to be most common among those who earnestly try to follow God) means waiting while we are doing all that we can to find his will — not parked with the brake on. Ask yourself, "Am I stationary with the engine (brain) turned off? Or am I actively using the abilities God has given me so that God can steer my thinking?" God does not speak into a vacuum. Is our mind a vacuum?

Step Three: Ask — and receive a reply.

Now for step three. "Ask and it will be given to you." These are the words of Jesus and you would think that everyone would take advantage of such an offer. Sadly, it is often the last thing attempted when seeking God's will. Those who are desperate find wisdom in their desperation and attempt this much earlier by saying, "Lord, help me!" Good thinking!

The word that does not occur in Jesus' statement and in most of his teaching about prayer (but is assumed) is the most important word: believe. When we ask we must believe that he will answer. If not, why do we ask?

But also, let your belief develop into an active anticipation. "I guess he will answer me," is hardly expectation. Do you check

23

expectantly to see if the heavenly e-mail has arrived? Or are you so distracted with yourself, your pain or joy and your world that you fail to check your heavenly mail? Anticipation of a response should rank up there with your excitement over the possible arrival of a lover's letter.

I have also met those who keep asking for God's help in an attempt to move heaven and earth but never even think to check their mailbox. The answer has often already arrived and awaits opening while they keep franticly asking. Sounds foolish, but this kind of faith that lacks expectancy and does not act according to its requests is common in the "faith with doubt" community.

Where is the mailbox? Ah, that's the million-dollar question for inexperienced recipients of heavenly mail. It's the still small voice in your mind and heart, most often. Consult your mind and heart for indications of God's voice.

It often comes into our minds in the form of a growing conviction that you are recognizing as the sound of God's voice. On the one hand, it may be something you didn't want to hear, but you just know that this persistent feeling is the right answer. Or it may be something you wanted to hear, and now you know that you are not leading your thoughts with your desires but recognizing the voice of God in your desires. The mailbox is in your own head where your mind and heart reside. Feelings (emotions) are generated in your brain — or at least observable there to modern science.

Special Delivery

"Special delivery" happens in dreams and voices audible to you
or via the words of a fellow pilgrim (to name a few of the
many alternative ways God communicates). Don't become
obsessed with every feeling you happen to have as though it is
a special delivery. Special delivery is clearly marked. It will
jump out at you. Just be aware of what is happening to you
and pay attention to anything that may be an answer to your
requests.

A dream that just happens "out of the blue" is probably just
another night's meandering of the subconscious, unless it is
accompanied by that undeniable conviction that only you can
know. That is, that it is from the Holy Spirit of God to your
spirit. It's the conviction that comes stamped "Special
Delivery." And if you need more in the way of reassurance,
then use the "tests" with which I will end.

My Desires — How to handle them

A word about desires...
Don't label them always as suspicious. Even though desires
can be deceptive and we can focus on them so powerfully as
to convince ourselves that what we want is God's will, they
can also be a first mailing of God's will to us — an awakening
of a slumbering desire. If the desire is from God, it is often
sent as motivation to act. The development of a passion in our
hearts (one that Jesus could sign his name to) is sometimes

God's way of encouraging us to proceed and a revelation of his will.

The trick in deciphering which is a message from God, or which is a selfish craving, is to listen carefully for the telltale signs that the desire is simply our own attempt to get what we want. Those signs come most often in the form of an uncomfortable feeling that just won't go away, a feeling that this is not right. Or the sign may be in a more obvious form: that of knowing that it isn't what Jesus would do. Or it may be the realization that the super effort I'm putting into getting this prayer approved is in itself suspicious.

The detection of selfishness is, again, usually made by the presence of that uncomfortable feeling I just mentioned. And selfishness can be detected by the tests that I have kept promising you. They're coming!

How Asking and Believing Can Become Certain Guidance

This step of asking and believing is the only way to be really sure of God's will.

Let me spell this out carefully, even laboriously, as it is most important. The only way to be really sure that you have found Gods' will is to ask, believe that you have been or will be given the answer, and act on your faith that God will lead you as you follow what you perceive to be his leading (and stop you or redirect you if you are wrong). That's God-confident asking in a nutshell. It's our way of walking though life with absolute certainty — by faith. Faith is the only certainty we have in this life. "Faith is the substance of things hoped for, the evidence of things not seen," Hebrews 11:1.

When Jesus was talking about not being anxious — about how God cares for the sparrow and how he will care much more for you — he was endeavoring to get us to live by faith. Just ask and believe that you will get the answer to your prayer. God will then guide you and all you have to do is walk confidently until he gets your attention and redirects you! Got it?

If you are still apprehensive and you know it is not a matter of your doubting God, then ask again and check the mailbox regularly. Doubting yourself and your ability to decipher God's voice warrants making another request, but not if you are doubting God! In that case another request is futile spinning of a prayer wheel.

There are those who ask constantly and are never confident of an answer. They continually put it down to their questioning of themselves. "Did I really hear God's voice?" they say. Such a lack of faith could point to low self-esteem or some blockage that has them stranded in doubts dark territory. Check with your clergy or trusted counselor. But in short, the answer should be clear. God will, I say *will*, lead you. Just believe it and proceed. He will do to you what he did to Paul if you are honestly a seeker after his will. He will stop you if, and where, needed. Find the courage to believe.

Please, whatever you do, live by faith. You will never be able to live with certainty, using knowledge as your guide, because you will never know all the facts. Remember, we are limited creatures. Only God knows all the facts and can unerringly guide you.

Ask and you will receive. There is no easier or more reliable way to find God's will. But remember: he may not answer until you have done your homework. (The vehicle must be moving to be steered).

Let me repeat again for emphasis: He always answers either positively, negatively or by our least favorite response, namely, "Wait." Patience can be, and is at times, the total answer to our request, as it often contains the developing bud of new growth that we need to experience before God can lead us any further.

Step Four: Sanctioned tests

Step Four is to apply the tests.

<u>Test number one: "Is this answer one I would expect from a Holy God?"</u>
You can do this simple exercise in your mind by calling to memory what you know about God and his ways and, therefore, test your conclusion. It's an excellent method and

one of the reasons the psalmist insisted that we "Hide God's word in your heart so that you may not sin against Him." Carrying the Bible in your heart is the safest way to carry your Bible and the best. And if you don't have it in your heart, start by filling your mind with the reading of the life and teachings of Jesus.

Test number two is also sanctioned by the Bible.
Ask a wise person for counsel — preferably one who you know to be wise in the counsel of God's wisdom. This person is usually not a close friend who does not want to fall out of favor with you. It is someone who will tell you what you need to hear.

These tests will hopefully save you from falling into the trap of believing what you want to believe instead of finding God's will for your life. But, there is still one more test — my favorite.

Test number three: Consult the Referee
Test number three is the peace of God. Philippians, Chapter 4, verse 7 says, "… and the peace of God which surpasses all understanding [God's peace is always better than the obsession of having to understand] will guard your hearts and minds…" This is a comforting word picture that can become a successful procedure in all difficult decisions that you may face.

The Greek word translated by the word "guard" is a word the Greeks used for an umpire at a sports event. The umpire calls the play fair or foul, in or out, or records all infringements of the rules. In this case, the umpire is the Peace of God. Every decision in your life is called right or wrong by this umpire. Breaches of the rules are "heard" by the raucous din of self-centered opinions and disturbing feelings — the opposite of peace from God. It's the peace of God that unerringly brings certitude that the decision was indeed right on plan. Of course, even this test is subject to your unwavering faith in this promise of God.

So, in the matter of discerning God's guidance in your life, let me rephrase the verse in the form of a spiritual exercise.

First, weigh all the facts related to your decision that are known to you and come to your best honest decision. Preferably write it down. This is doing your homework.

Then, before you go to bed, pray and ask God to confirm or reject your decision by giving you or not giving you, when you wake up in the morning an unmistakable peace about your decision (the peace of God in your heart). If the decision you made the night before is in line with his plan, he will give you his peace in your heart — an unmistakable feeling of goodness and calm. If you have no peace, abandon your decision. You got it wrong.

Act in faith. You have made your best decision and have activated God's promise to you. Believe the results. Is God not bound to answer according to his promise? All major decisions in my life have been made this way and I have yet to find in hindsight that any were mistakes. Do you think we will make a mistake relying on God's promise to us?

Live confidently, happily in the center of God's will. Live by faith.

Note: To whom it may concern. Although, in these pages, I use the traditional masculine pronoun to refer to God, it should be understood that, in our human terms, he is both male and female since both male and female were created in his image — another way of saying that it takes both male and female to represent the image of God. He is also called both Father and Mother in the Bible. The gender of God is really a non-issue since when using gender we are trying to represent him in terms that we are familiar with — human terms, not the real terms under which he exists and lives, which are divine terms of which we have no direct knowledge.

About the Author

Ray Lincoln has served as senior pastor to single and multi-staffed churches in New Zealand, Australia and the USA. His 50 plus years of experience in coaching, counseling and teaching have given him the opportunity to guide many people to self-discovery and spiritual renewal. He has studied extensively in the areas of Temperament/Psychology, Theology, Philosophy and Neuroscience and has earned a BA, BD, MDiv, PhD and LTh.

Teaching people to succeed in life and overcome their challenges with God's strength are his passion. Ray says, "While remaining true to the teachings of the Bible, my strong interest has been to use the best of science and develop a true Biblical Psychology that can help people find true fulfillment. God wants this for all of us. He knows best how we function and has left us the most helpful life-manual in the best-selling book ever!"

Conducting hundreds of seminars in Australia, New Zealand and the USA has led him to lecture in universities, seminaries, and Bible colleges as well as businesses and churches. He has mentored pastors and other professionals. Ray has a deep faith in God, strengthened by his studies, and offers his services, experience and knowledge to you. His wife, Mary Jo, is more than a willing partner in his ministry and, in her own right, contributes much to their joint mission.